Fundamentals of the FAITH

*A*ll Scripture is inspired

by God and profitable

for teaching, for reproof,

for correction, for training

in righteousness.

2 Timothy 3:16

Fundamentals of the Faith
Revised Edition

Grace Community Church
13248 Roscoe Blvd.
Sun Valley, CA 91352
(800) 472-2315

Printed in the United States of America

All Scripture quotations, except those noted otherwise, are from the *New American Standard Bible,* © 1960, 1962, 1963, 1968, 1971, 1972, 1973, 1975, 1977 by The Lockman Foundation. Used by permission.

The Bible-at-a-Glance chart (Lesson 1) is from *The Spirit-Filled Christian,* © 1973, 1980 by The Navigators. Used by permission of the publisher.

Five-Methods-of-Scripture-Intake illustration (Lesson 2) is from *The Spirit-Filled Christian,* © 1973, 1980 by The Navigators. Used by permission of the publisher.

Quote by A.W. Tozer (Lesson 3) is from *The Knowledge of the Holy* by A.W. Tozer, © 1961 by Aidan Wilson Tozer. Used by permission of HarperCollins Publishers Inc.

Quote on righteousness (Lesson 3) is from *The Zondervan Pictorial Encyclopedia of the Bible,* Volume 5. Merrill C. Tenney, General Editor. © 1975, 1976 by The Zondervan Corporation. Used by permission of the publisher.

Definition of *grace* by John MacArthur (Lesson 6) is from *The John MacArthur New Testament Commentary: Galatians.* © 1987 by Moody Press. Used by permission of the publisher.

Definition of a seal (Lesson 7) is from *The Zondervan Pictorial Encyclopedia of the Bible,* Volume 5. Merrill C. Tenney, General Editor. ©1975, 1976 by The Zondervan Corporation. Used by permission of the publisher.

Quotes by John MacArthur on the filling of the Holy Spirit (Lesson 7) are from *The John MacArthur New Testament Commentary: Ephesians.* ©1986 by Moody Press. Used by permission of the publisher.

Quote by John MacArthur on the church (Lesson 9) is from *Body Dynamics.* © 1982 by Scripture Press. Used by permission of the publisher.

ISBN 1-883973-01-5

Contents

Introduction

On Sunday mornings at Grace Community Church, small groups of people gather in *Fundamentals of the Faith (FOF)* classes to use this manual of thirteen lessons, which blend basic biblical truths with personal obedience and service. The small group environment encourages interaction between the teacher and student and often results in the class members and teacher's being spiritually knit together. By the time FOF classes conclude, many lasting relationships have been formed. It has been a joy to see many, as a result of taking these classes, trust Christ as Lord and Savior. Many young believers also take these classes to grow in their understanding of biblical truths.

You may have wondered why this edition is softcover with pages perforated and three-hole-punched. The softcover simply makes the manual more affordable. Perforating the pages allows the teacher to make thirteen homework assignments and grade each lesson that the students turn in. The three-hole-punch allows the student to keep his or her lesson in a notebook.

Each year the FOF ministry reaches hundreds of people at Grace Community Church and thousands of people in many churches and languages around the world. As a result, many have grown in the grace and knowledge of our Lord. May this manual help you to do the same.

Introduction to the Bible

Lesson 1 Homework

Memorize: 2 Timothy 3:16

"All Scripture is inspired by God and profitable for teaching, for reproof, for correction, for training in righteousness."

2 Timothy 3:16

The Bible is the Word of God. It claims to be truth, the message from God to man. Second Peter 1:21 says that men "moved by the Holy Spirit spoke from God."

- ◆ The Scriptures were written by approximately forty different men.
- ◆ They lived in several different countries.
- ◆ They lived at different times (1400 B.C. to A.D. 90).
- ◆ They wrote in three languages: Hebrew, Aramaic, and Greek.

Despite this vast variety, God moved the writers to focus on God's glory in man's redemption with one central figure--Jesus Christ, the Son of God.

I. The Old Testament (39 books)

A. The Pentateuch (5 books)

The first five books of the Old Testament were written around 1400 B.C. by Moses. They are often referred to as the "Five Books of Moses," or the "Pentateuch."

List them below in the order you find them in your Bible:

1. _____ The book of beginnings: creation, man, sin, redemption, God's nation.

2. _____ God delivers His people from Egypt.

3. _____ Priestly laws on holiness and worship through sacrifice and purification.

4. _____ God's people continually disobey and wander in the wilderness for forty years.

5. _____ Moses' great discourses to prepare the people to enter the Promised Land.

B. Historical (12 books)

The historical books were written around 1400-450 B.C. and describe God's dealings with His chosen people, Israel, the Hebrew nation.

List these books in order:

1. _____ 5. _____ 9. _____

2. _____ 6. _____ 10. _____

3. _____ 7. _____ 11. _____

4. _____ 8. _____ 12. _____

C. Poetic (5 books)

The following five books are poetic, describing in poetry and song God's greatness and His dealings with men.

List these books in order:

1. _____ The suffering and loyal trust of a man who loved God.

2. _____ Songs of praise and instruction.

3. _____ God's practical wisdom for daily life.

4. _____ The emptiness of an earthly life without God.

5. _____ A portrait of God's love.

D. Major Prophets (5 books)

A prophet is one who is commissioned by God to deliver His message to men. These books are called "Major Prophets" because they are generally longer than the writings of the "Minor Prophets." They were written from approximately 750 to 550 B.C.

List these books in order:

1. _____ 4. _____

2. _____ 5. _____

3. _____

E. Minor Prophets (12 books)

The last twelve books of the Old Testament were written from approximately 840 B.C. to 400 B.C.

List these books in order:

1. _____   5. _____   9. _____

2. _____   6. _____   10. _____

3. _____   7. _____   11. _____

4. _____   8. _____   12. _____

II. The New Testament (27 books)

The New Testament, or New Covenant, reveals Jesus Christ, the Redeemer of men. In it we find:

- ◆ The life of Christ
- ◆ The way of salvation
- ◆ The beginning of Christianity
- ◆ Instruction for Christian living
- ◆ God's plan for the future

A. Historical (5 books)

1. The Gospels (first 4 books)

a. _____ The life of Christ, written especially for the Jews, revealing Jesus Christ as their long-awaited Messiah.

b. _____ The life of Christ, revealing Jesus as the obedient Servant of God. The book was written to the Roman world.

c. _____ The life of Christ, revealing Jesus as the perfect man, emphasizing His humanity. It was written by Luke, a Greek, to the Greek world.

d. _____ The life of Christ, revealing Jesus as the Son of God, stressing His deity. This book was written to all men.

Note: What two reasons are given for the writing of John's gospel (John 20:31)?

1. _____

_____

2. _____

_____

2. History of the Early Church (1 book)

List it:_____ The beginning and spread of the Christian church. It could be called the "Acts of the Holy Spirit," and was written as an evangelistic tool.

B. Letters or Epistles (21 books)

These books were written to individuals, to churches, or believers in general. The letters deal with every aspect of Christian faith and responsibility.

List them in order:

1. Paul's Letters (13 books)

a. _____   h. _____

b. _____   i. _____

c. _____   j. _____

d. _____   k. _____

e. _____   l. _____

f. _____   m. _____

g. _____

2. General Letters (8 books)

a. _____ e. _____

b. _____ f. _____

c. _____ g. _____

d. _____ h. _____

C. Prophecy (1 book)

The last book of the New Testament tells of future events:

◆ Return of Jesus Christ
◆ Reign of Jesus Christ
◆ Glory of Jesus Christ
◆ Future state of believers and unbelievers

This book is called _____.

III. Christ in the Bible

A. The Old and New Testaments are to be seen together and portray Jesus Christ as the central figure.

Read the following verses and complete the following phrases:

1. Luke 24:27. Christ is seen in _____.

2. John 5:39. Jesus said the Scriptures "bear witness of _____."

B. The key is Jesus.

5 Books of the Law	12 Historical Books	5 Poetic Books	17 Prophetic Books	4 Gospels	1 Acts	21 Letters	1 Revelation
Promises of Christ	Anticipation of Christ: Types, Experiences, Prophecies			Manifestation of Christ	The Church of Christ		Coronation of Christ

IV. Why Is the Bible Important?

When tempted by Satan, Jesus alluded to Deuteronomy 8:3, "Man shall not live on bread alone, but on every word that proceeds out of the mouth of God" (Matthew 4:4).

A. What does 2 Timothy 3:16 say about the Bible?
   (Circle the correct answer.)

   1. Some of the Bible is inspired by God.
   2. There are a few parts which are not inspired.
   3. All of the Bible is inspired by God.
   4. Only those parts which speak to us in a personal way are inspired by God.

B. How do the following verses show the importance of God's Word?

   1. 2 Timothy 3:15 _____

   _____

   _____

   2. Hebrews 4:12 _____

   _____

   _____

C. What four things does God's Word do?

   1. Psalm 19:7a _____

   2. Psalm 19:7b _____

   3. Psalm 19:8a _____

   4. Psalm 19:8b _____

V. Application

Based on what you have learned about the Bible, what should be your response?

_____

_____

_____

_____

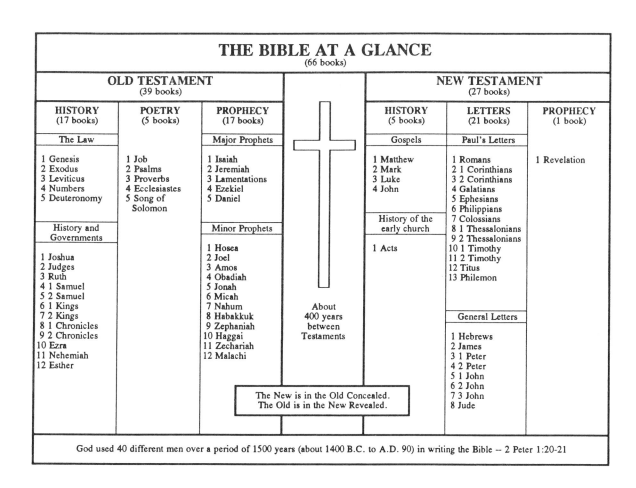

THE BIBLE AT A GLANCE
(66 books)

OLD TESTAMENT (39 books)				NEW TESTAMENT (27 books)		
HISTORY (17 books)	**POETRY** (5 books)	**PROPHECY** (17 books)		**HISTORY** (5 books)	**LETTERS** (21 books)	**PROPHECY** (1 book)
The Law		Major Prophets		Gospels	Paul's Letters	1 Revelation
1 Genesis 2 Exodus 3 Leviticus 4 Numbers 5 Deuteronomy	1 Job 2 Psalms 3 Proverbs 4 Ecclesiastes 5 Song of Solomon	1 Isaiah 2 Jeremiah 3 Lamentations 4 Ezekiel 5 Daniel		1 Matthew 2 Mark 3 Luke 4 John	1 Romans 2 1 Corinthians 3 2 Corinthians 4 Galatians 5 Ephesians 6 Philippians 7 Colossians 8 1 Thessalonians 9 2 Thessalonians 10 1 Timothy 11 2 Timothy 12 Titus 13 Philemon	
History and Governments		Minor Prophets		History of the early church		
1 Joshua 2 Judges 3 Ruth 4 1 Samuel 5 2 Samuel 6 1 Kings 7 2 Kings 8 1 Chronicles 9 2 Chronicles 10 Ezra 11 Nehemiah 12 Esther		1 Hosea 2 Joel 3 Amos 4 Obadiah 5 Jonah 6 Micah 7 Nahum 8 Habakkuk 9 Zephaniah 10 Haggai 11 Zechariah 12 Malachi	About 400 years between Testaments	1 Acts	General Letters	
					1 Hebrews 2 James 3 1 Peter 4 2 Peter 5 1 John 6 2 John 7 3 John 8 Jude	

The New is in the Old Concealed.
The Old is in the New Revealed.

God used 40 different men over a period of 1500 years (about 1400 B.C. to A.D. 90) in writing the Bible — 2 Peter 1:20-21

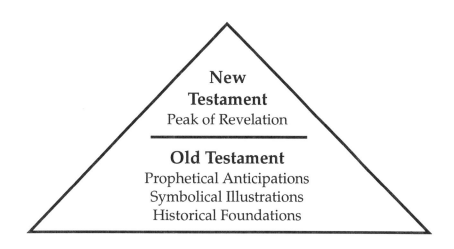

New Testament
Peak of Revelation

Old Testament
Prophetical Anticipations
Symbolical Illustrations
Historical Foundations

How the Bible Became Ours

```
┌─────────────────────────────────────────────┐
│              Original Manuscripts             │
│        from Around 1500 B.C. to A.D. 100      │
│   Sixty-six distinct works. Some writers unknown. │
└─────────────────────────────────────────────┘
```

┌─────────────────────────────────────┐   ┌─────────────────────────────────────┐
│ Manuscripts in original language.   │   │ Translations into other languages and │
│   │   │   quotations.   │
└─────────────────────────────────────┘   └─────────────────────────────────────┘

A.D.385-404: The Vulgate, Jerome's Latin translation.

A.D.700-1000: Various Anglo-Saxon partial translations.

A.D.1382: Complete translations by John Wycliffe and followers.

A.D.1525-1535: First printed translation by William Tyndale

1535: Coverdale's translation; 1537: Matthew's; 1539: Taverner's and Great Bible
translation; 1560: Geneva Bible; 1568: Bishop's; 1610: Rheim's-Douai

A.D.1611: The King James Version

— *More Discoveries* ⟶

1885: English Revised Version

1901: American Standard Version

1947: Dead Sea Scrolls

1952: Revised Standard Version; 1960: New American Standard Version;

1966: The Jerusalem Bible; 1971: Living Bible (Paraphrase); 1973: The Common Bible;

1973: New International Bible

How to Know the Bible

Lesson 2 Homework

Memorize: 2 Timothy 2:15

"Be diligent to present yourself approved to God as a workman who does not need to be ashamed, handling accurately the word of truth."

2 Timothy 2:15

The "how" of learning and applying the Scripture to life is something every Christian should know. This lesson covers five ways to make the Bible yours: hearing, reading, studying, memorizing, and meditating.

Compare those five methods of learning Scripture to the fingers on your hand. If you hold the Bible with only two fingers, it is easy to lose your grip. But as you use more fingers, your grasp of the Bible becomes stronger.

That is also true spiritually. If a person hears, reads, studies, memorizes, and then meditates on the Bible, his grasp of the truths of the Bible becomes firm and part of his life. As the thumb is needed in combination with any finger to complete your hold, so meditation combined with hearing, reading, studying, and memorizing is essential for a full grasp of God's Word.

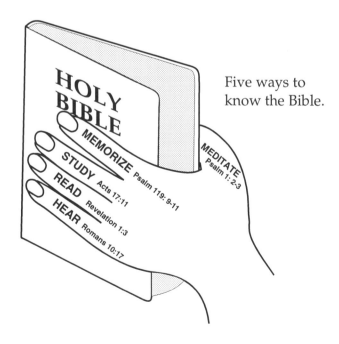

Five ways to know the Bible.

I. Reasons for Understanding the Bible

List five reasons for knowing God's Word:

A. 2 Timothy 2:15 _____

B. 1 Peter 2:2 _____

C. Psalm 119:11 _____

D. Psalm 119:38 _____

E. Psalm 119:105 _____

We study the Scripture because it is sufficient.

"All Scripture is inspired by God and profitable for teaching, for reproof, for correction, for training in righteousness."
                                        2 Timothy 3:16

II. How to Know the Bible

A. Hear It

"So faith comes from hearing, and hearing by the word of Christ" (Romans 10:17).

1. Whom did Jesus say would be blessed (Luke 11:28)?

_____

2. In proclaiming the Word, what should pastors and teachers do (Nehemiah 8:7-8)?

_____

B. Read It

"Blessed is he who reads and those who hear the words of the prophecy, and heed the things which are written in it; for the time is near" (Revelation 1:3).

1. Write Revelation 1:3 in your own words: _____

_____

2. To what did Paul ask Timothy to give his attention (1 Timothy 4:13)?

_____

If you do not have a daily reading plan, start with the gospel of Mark or John. At the rate of two chapters each day, you will complete the New Testament in nineteen weeks!

C. Study It

When the Apostle Paul left Thessalonica, he came to Berea and shared the gospel with unbelieving Jews. What he found was that they "were more noble-minded than those in Thessalonica, for they received the word with great eagerness, examining the Scriptures daily, to see whether these things were so" (Acts 17:11).

Attitudes toward Bible study:

1. From Acts 17:11, how did the Bereans receive the Word of God?

_____

2. How should we search after wisdom or understanding (Proverbs 2:4)?

_____

> **Bible study is more than just reading the Bible; it involves careful observation, interpretation, and application. Reading gives you the overall picture, but study helps you think, learn, and apply what you read to your life.**

D. Memorize It

> *"How can a young man keep his way pure? By keeping it according to Thy word.... Thy word I have treasured in my heart, that I may not sin against Thee."*
> Psalm 119:9,11

1. How did God command Israel to remember His Word?

    a. Deuteronomy 11:18a _____

    b. Deuteronomy 11:19 _____

2. Read Matthew 4:4,7,10.

    a. During the three confrontations with Satan, what did Jesus do to overcome

    His temptations? _____

    _____

b. How might you apply this example to your own life? _____

_____

3. Write Psalm 40:8 in your own words: _____

_____

> **It is easier to memorize with a purpose. Understanding the meaning or application of the passage will make memorizing easier.**

E. Meditate On It

> *"How blessed is the man who does not walk in the counsel of the wicked, nor stand in the path of sinners, nor sit in the seat of scoffers! But his delight is in the law of the Lord, and in His law he **meditates day and night.** And he will be like a tree firmly planted by streams of water, which yields its fruit in its season, and its leaf does not wither; and in whatever he does, he prospers."*
>
> Psalm 1:1-3

> **Meditation is prayerful reflection on Scripture with a view toward understanding and application. Give prayerful thought to God's Word with the goal of conforming your life to His will.**

1. Meditation on Scripture can be done as you:

    a. Hear the Word preached.

    b. Read the Bible.

    c. Pray about what you are studying.

    d. Reflect on the verses you have memorized.

2. How does meditation assist you (Joshua 1:8)? _____

_____

12

3. Do you think God's Word can affect your speech and actions? How (Luke 6:45)?

_____

4. Besides being diligent in learning God's Word, what else should we do in order to understand it (Psalm 119:73,125)?

_____

III. The Bible Study Process

A. STEP 1: PREPARATION

1. What should we do before we approach the Scriptures (1 Peter 2:1-2)?

_____

_____

2. What should be the content of our prayer as we prepare to study God's Word (Colossians 1:9-10)?

_____

> Spend a short time in prayer before each study. Confess any sin and ask for the Holy Spirit to
> _"open my eyes, that I may behold wonderful things from Thy law."_
> Psalm 119:18

B. STEP 2: OBSERVATION

Observation: _"What is taking place in the passage? What do I see?"_

1. Ask questions as you read; _write them down._ Who? What? Where? When?

2. As you observe the passage, look for:

   a. Key words

   b. Key subjects (people, topics)

   c. Commands

d. Warnings

e. Repeated words or phrases

f. Lists of things

g. Comparisons (things that are similar; things that are different)

h. Questions, answers given

i. Anything unusual or unexpected

Note: These are just a few examples of things to look for when observing a passage.

Warning: Take your time! Don't give up too soon!

C. Step 3: Interpretation

1. *Interpretation: "What does it mean?"*

2. Scripture can be clear. Whom has God given to teach us (1 John 2:27)?

_____

3. Begin by asking interpretive questions:

a. What is the importance of...

(1) A given word (especially verbs)

(2) A given phrase

(3) Names and titles

(4) Dates

(5) Others?

b. What is the meaning of a particular word?

c. Why did the writer say this?

d. What is the implication of this word, phrase, or name?

4. To find answers to your interpretive questions, use:

a. The context, which is the verses before and after the passage you are studying.

b. Definitions of words

c. Grammar and sentence structure

d. Other passages of Scripture

e. Bible Study tools

    (1) Bible Dictionary

    (2) Concordance

    (3) Bible Handbook

    (4) Bible Encyclopedia

    (5) Bible Commentary

5. When interpreting, remember...

a. All Scripture will agree. It will not contradict itself.

b. Seek to let the passage speak for itself in its context. Be careful not to draw conclusions that the author did not intend.

> **There is only one correct interpretation of any particular passage of Scripture—the author's originally intended meaning.**

D. Step 4: APPLICATION

1. *Application: "What effect will this have on my life?"*

> **This part of the Bible study process takes the truths that have been observed and seeks to incorporate them into everyday life and practice.**

2. Once we have heard the Word of God, what should be our response (James 1:22)? _____

_____

3. A simple tool to help you apply what you have learned is to "put on the *SPECS*."

Is there a...

    S in to forsake?

    P romise to claim?

    E xample to follow?

    C ommand to obey?

    S tumbling block to avoid?

> **While there is only one correct interpretation of a given passage of Scripture, there are many applications.**

E. Bible Study is a repetitive process.

When studying a verse, steps 2, 3, and 4 are used over and over.

1. *Observe*, then *interpret*, then *apply*.

2. You may choose to do this for each word, phrase, or thought.

> **The more passes you make through the verse, the deeper its meaning is opened to you.**

IV. Study Exercise

> *"But seek first His kingdom and His righteousness; and all these things shall be added to you."*
>
>   Matthew 6:33

Using Matthew 6:33 (above)...

A. Make as many observations as you can, listing them in the **"Observations"** column on the next page.

B. Write interpretive questions about your observations.

C. Write the "meaning" of your observation in the **"Interpretations"** column.

D. Once you have completed your observations and interpretations, fill in the **"Application"** section.

Note: The first six have been done as examples.

Observations	Interpretive Questions	Interpretations
1. The verse starts with the conjunction *but*.	1. Why does the sentence start with *but*?	1. This verse is linked to the previous verses. Must read Matthew 6:31-32 for context.
2. Key word: *seek*	2. What does it mean? What action does *seek* require?	2. It means to pursue or search. It is a command.
3. The verb *seek* is in the present tense.	3. What does present tense indicate?	3. I must seek now.
4. Note the use of the word *first* following *seek*.	4. What is the importance of *first*?	4. Implies priority. Must seek as a top priority.
5. Next key word is *kingdom*.	5. What does the word *kingdom* signify?	5. It is a sovereign rule or dominion over a specific realm or region.
6. The word *kingdom* is preceeded by the personal pronoun *His*.	6. Whose kingdom is identified? To whom does *His* refer?	6. Looking back to verse 32, *His* is "God the Father." It is God's kingdom.
7.	7.	7.
8.	8.	8.
9.	9.	9.
10.	10.	10.
11.	11.	11.
12.	12.	12.

Write out one application based on your observations and interpretations (refer to SPECS in the "Step 4: Application" section).

_____

_____

_____

V. Application

Are the *168 hours* in your week being invested well? Should you make any changes?

The following table will help you analyze your habits for making the Bible yours. As you fill in the number of hours spent per week, pray about setting any needed new goals.

Time in the word	My Present Program	New Goals and Plans
Hearing the Word		
Reading the Word		
Studying the Word		
Memorizing the Word		

God: His Character and Attributes
Lesson 3 Homework

Memorize: 1 Chronicles 29:11

"Thine, O Lord, is the greatness and the power and the glory and the victory and the majesty, indeed everything that is in the heavens and the earth; Thine is the dominion, O Lord, and Thou dost exalt Thyself as head over all."

1 Chronicles 29:11

I. Introduction

In the religions of today's world, there are many so-called gods and just as many opinions about what God (or god) is like. The Bible, on the other hand, claims to be the revelation of the one true God. The Bible never tries to prove God, it simply states, "In the beginning God" (Genesis 1:1).

"Plunge yourself in the Godhead's deepest sea; be lost in His immensity; and you shall come forth as from a couch of rest refreshed and invigorated. I know nothing which can so comfort the soul; so calm the swelling billows of sorrow and grief; so speak peace to the winds of trial, as a devout musing upon the subject of the Godhead."

C.H. Spurgeon on January 7, 1855

   A. According to Psalm 89:7-8, list two things true of God:

_____

_____

   B. What statement is made that points to the fact that there is only one God (Isaiah 43:10)?

_____

_____

_____

_____

   C. What is it that God will not give to another (Isaiah 42:8)?

_____

_____

II. The Importance of Knowing God

A. Jesus equated "knowing God" to what (John 17:3)?

_____

B. Rather than boasting in wisdom, might, or riches, what one thing does God say a man should boast about (Jeremiah 9:24)?

_____

> "A right conception of God is basic not only to systematic theology but to practical Christian living as well ... I believe there is scarcely an error in doctrine or a failure in applying Christian ethics that cannot be traced finally to imperfect and ignoble thoughts about God."
>
> A.W. Tozer

III. How Can One Know God?

A. What does Jesus say about the means for knowing God (John 14:8-9)?

_____

B. What does Paul say about Christ in Colossians 2:9?

_____

C. The writer of Hebrews says that God has spoken to us in His Son. How does he describe Him (Hebrews 1:3)?

_____

_____

IV. God's Attributes

A. An "attribute" is a quality or characteristic that is true about someone. Studying the attributes of God allows us to have a limited understanding of God's Person. Even though some concepts exceed the limits of our comprehension, our ideas concerning God need to be as true as possible.

Father, Son, and Holy Spirit	
1. Holiness	6. Omniscience
2. Righteousness and Justice	7. Omnipresence
	8. Omnipotence
3. Sovereignty	9. Love
4. Eternality	10. Truth
5. Immutability	11. Mercy
Note: These are just a few of God's attributes.	

B. God's Attributes Defined

First: Look up the Scripture listed with the following attributes, then write down the part of the verse that best describes the given attribute.

Second: Based on your understanding of each attribute, write out how that personally applies to you.

1. Holiness

God's attribute of holiness means that He is untouched and unstained by the evil in the world. He is absolutely pure and perfect.

a. Exodus 15:11 _____

_____

b. Psalm 99:9 _____

_____

_____

Because God is holy, we are exhorted to be holy (1 Peter 1:16). We are to be set apart from sin unto God. Our lives are to shine as a reflection of God in an unrighteous world.

Personal Application: _____

_____

_____

_____

2. Righteousness and Justice

Righteousness and *justice* are derived from the same root word in the original language of the New Testament. The meaning is that of being "right" or "just."

Righteousness designates the perfect agreement between God's nature and His acts. Justice is the way in which God legislates His righteousness. There is no action that God takes in relation to man that violates any code of morality or justice.

> " There is no law **above** God, but there is a law **in** God."
> "Righteousness," *The Zondervan Pictorial Encyclopedia of the Bible*

a. According to Psalm 119:137, God's righteousness is displayed in His upright

_____.

b. According to Psalm 89:14, righteousness and justice are referred to as

_____.

How does *your standard* of what is right and just compare with *God's standard?*

Personal Application: _____

_____

_____

_____

_____

3. Sovereignty

The word *sovereign* means chief or highest; supreme in power; superior in position to all others.

a. Isaiah 46:9-10 _____

_____

b. Isaiah 45:23 _____

The idea of sovereignty is an encouraging one, for it assures the Christian that nothing is out of God's control and that His plans cannot be thwarted (Romans 8:28).

Personal Application: _____

_____

_____

_____

_____

4. Eternality

Since God is eternal, there has never been a time when God did not exist. He had no beginning and will have no end.

a. Isaiah 44:6 _____

_____

b. Isaiah 43:13 _____

Being eternal, God is not bound by time. Having always existed, He sees the past and the future as clearly as He sees the present. With that perspective, He has a perfect understanding of what is best for our lives. Therefore, we should trust Him with all areas of our lives.

Personal Application: _____

_____

_____

_____

5. Immutability

God never changes in His nature or purpose.

a. Malachi 3:6 _____

_____

b. Hebrews 6:17-18 _____

_____

The Bible contains numerous promises for those who belong to Him. God can be trusted to keep His Word.

Personal Application: _____

_____

_____

6. Omniscience

God knows all things possible and actual. Nothing takes Him by surprise.

a. Job 34:21 _____

_____

b. Psalm 139:1-6 _____

_____

If God is omniscient, then He knew all of our sins (past, present, and future) at the time of our salvation. Yet, He still forgave us and received us into His family forever. What does that say about the security of our salvation?

Personal Application: _____

_____

_____

_____

7. Omnipresence

God is present everywhere in the universe.

a. Proverbs 15:3 _____

_____

b. Psalm 139:7-12 _____

If God is everywhere, it is foolish to think we can hide from Him. However, it also means that a believer may experience the presence of God at all times and know the blessings of walking with Him.

Personal Application: _____

_____

_____

8. Omnipotence

God is all-powerful, having more than enough strength to do anything.

a. Jeremiah 32:17 _____

_____

b. Revelation 19:6 _____

_____

God's omnipotence is seen in:

◆ His power to create (Genesis 1:1)

◆ His preservation of all things (Hebrews 1:3)

◆ His providential care for us Psalm (37:23-24)

What can you learn from Isaiah 41:10 about God's omnipotence?

> *"Do not fear, for I am with you; do not anxiously look about you, for I am your God. I will strengthen you, surely I will help you, surely I will uphold you with My righteous right hand."*
>
> Isaiah 41:10

Personal Application: _____

_____

_____

9. Love

God is love. His love is unconditional; it is not based on the loveliness or merit of the object.

a. John 3:16 _____

_____

b. Romans 5:8 _____

_____

Love expresses itself in *action*. God is our example. He demonstrated His love for us in sending Jesus to die in our place (2 Corinthians 5:21).

Personal Application: _____

_____

_____

10. Truth

God is the only true God.

a. Psalm 31:5 _____

_____

b. Psalm 117:2 _____

_____

God's truth is above all. He is truthful even if all men are found to be liars. Therefore, His words and His judgments always prevail (Romans 3:4).

In light of that, how should you view God's Word and the truths contained in it?

Personal Application: _____

_____

_____

11. Mercy

God's great mercy is the practical expression of His compassion to those who have opposed His will.

a. Psalm 145:8-9 _____

_____

_____

b. Psalm 130:3-4 _____

God's great mercy is contrasted with man's sin. His mercy is displayed in our salvation (Ephesians 2:4-5).

Personal Application: _____

_____

_____

V. Application

In light of the attributes of God discussed in this lesson, answer the following questions:

A. How will your prayers be affected? _____

_____

_____

B. How would you respond to a major trial in your life such as:

1. The death of a close relative (spouse, child)?

2. An accident that leaves you physically disabled?

_____

_____

_____

_____

The Person of Jesus Christ

Lesson 4: Homework

> Memorize: John 1:1,14
>
> *"In the beginning was the Word, and the Word was with God, and the Word was God.... And the Word became flesh, and dwelt among us, and we beheld His glory, glory as of the only begotten from the Father, full of grace and truth."*
>
> John 1:1,14

Jesus Christ is the central figure of all human history. There has never been anyone like Him. He is regarded as a great teacher, a religious leader, a prophet, the Son of God, even God Himself. The claims He made, as well as those that others have made about Him, have propelled Him into the center of endless controversies throughout man's history. Wars have been fought about Him; countries have divided over Him; masses of His followers have given their lives for Him. Who is this man called "Jesus?"

Pontius Pilate unwittingly summed it up when he said, "Then what shall I do with Jesus who is called Christ" (Matthew 27:22)? Before anyone can answer that question for himself, he must first understand who Jesus is. This lesson will introduce Him to you.

I. The God Who Became Man

Jesus Christ came into the world in human flesh. By coming into the world as a man, He voluntarily set aside the independent use of His divine attributes and took on the form of a man. He was fully human, a man in every way, except He was without sin. This is referred to as the "incarnation."

A. What does Philippians 2:6 say about Jesus before He was born?

_____

B. According to Philippians 2:7, what did Jesus do?

_____

_____

29

C. Jesus was a man like us.

   1. Describe Jesus' human growth and development as a youth (Luke 2:40, 52).

     _____

   2. What was Jesus' response when He was tired (Mark 4:38)?

     _____

   3. What was Jesus' response to the lack of food (Luke 4:2)?

     _____

   4. How did Jesus feel after a journey (John 4:6)?

     _____

   5. How did Jesus react when He was grieved (John 11:35)?

     _____

   6. What did Jesus say about Himself (Luke 24:39)?

     _____

II. The Man Who Is God

Even though Jesus took on the form of a man, He was still fully God. Consider the following marks of "deity" attributed to Christ:

A. Attributes

Look up the following verses which describe these attributes of Christ:
Sovereign... Matthew 28:18
Eternal .... 1 John 1:1-2
Unchanging (immutable) .... Hebrews 13:8
All-Knowing (omniscient) .... Colossians 2:2b-3
Perfect or Sinless .... 2 Corinthians 5:21
Holy .... Acts 3:14-15
Truth .... John 14:6

Christ demonstrated His power (omnipotence) in His earthly ministry in the following ways:

1. Matthew 8:23-27 Power over _____

2. Luke 4:40 Power over _____

3. Luke 4:33-36 Power over _____

4. John 11:43-44 Power over _____

What additional authority did Jesus claim and exercise (Mark 2:3-12)?

_____(verse 10)

According to Mark 2:7, who alone can forgive sin? _____

If Jesus had the authority to forgive sins, and only God can forgive sins,

then who is Jesus Christ? _____!

B. Titles of Deity

1. Matthew 1:23 _____ (God with us)

2. Philippians 2:10-11 _____ (Sovereign)

3. John 8:58 _____ (Title reserved for God, Exodus 3:14)

C. Statements of Deity (Write out the key statement)

1. Colossians 2:9 _____

_____

2. Hebrews 1:1-3a _____

_____

3. John 1:1,14: Jesus Christ ("The Word") is _____

4. Titus 2:13 _____

III. The Christ Who Is Savior

According to John 3:17, Jesus is the Savior of the world. List the following titles that describe God's saving grace:

A. John 1:29 _____

B. John 6:35 _____

C. John 14:6 _____

IV. The King Who Comes to Rule

Jesus is not just a Person of the past. He is the destined King of kings and Lord of lords (1 Timothy 6:14-15) who will someday reign over all the earth.

A. What three things has Christ been given (Daniel 7:14)?

1. _____

2. _____

3. _____

B. What did Jesus tell His followers in Matthew 25:31-32?

_____

_____

_____

C. When Christ ascended into heaven forty days after the resurrection, what were the apostles told (Acts 1:11)?

_____

D. Describe the return of Jesus Christ (2 Thessalonians 1:7b-10).

_____

_____

_____

V. Application

In light of who Christ is:

- ◆ God
- ◆ Savior
- ◆ King/Ruler

A. How can you best prepare for His second coming (2 Peter 3:14)?

_____

_____

_____

B. What can you do this week to acknowledge who He is (Revelation 5:11-14)?

_____

_____

_____

The Work of Christ
Lesson 5 Homework

Memorize: 1 Corinthians 15:3-4

"For I delivered to you as of first importance what I also received, that Christ died for our sins according to the Scriptures, and that He was buried, and that He was raised on the third day according to the Scriptures."

1 Corinthians 15:3-4

The Scriptures tell us that, "He Himself bore our sins in His body on the cross, that we might die to sin and live to righteousness" (1 Peter 2:24).

I. Man's Need for Christ's Work

A. According to Romans 3:10-12, of what six things is every man guilty?

1. _____

2. _____

3. _____

4. _____

5. _____

6. _____

Romans 3:23 sums up the problem, "For all have sinned and fall short of the glory of God."

B. To what is man a slave (John 8:34)? _____

C. What is the end result of sin (James 1:15)? _____

D. Because we were dead in trespasses and sins, whom did we follow and what kind of children were we (Ephesians 2:1-3)?

_____

_____

E. Whose wrath will the "sons of disobedience" experience (Ephesians 5:6)?

_____

Will God Tolerate Sin?

"Cursed is everyone who does not abide by all things written in the book of the Law, to perform them."

Galatians 3:10

As we studied in Lesson 3, God will assert His holiness and demands conformity to that holiness. Man is faced with:

- ◆ Sin. . . . . Romans 3:23
- ◆ Having God as His enemy . . . . James 4:4b
- ◆ Subjection to the power of Satan . . . . 1 John 5:19
- ◆ Being helpless to save himself. . . . . Romans 5:6
- ◆ Facing death . . . . Romans 6:23
- ◆ Condemnation and eternal separation from God . . . 2 Thessalonians 1:9

II. The Cost of Christ's Work

A. Read Philippians 2:7-8

1. What are three things Christ did when He came to earth (verse 7)?

   a. _____

   b. _____

   c. _____

2. In what way did Jesus humble Himself (verse 8)?

_____

B. What happened to Jesus on earth according to Isaiah 53:3?

_____

_____

C. Forgiveness of sins requires what (Hebrews 9:22)?

_____

D. What price did Christ pay to redeem us (1 Peter 1:18-19)?

_____

E. What did Jesus cry out on the cross? Why (Matthew 27:46)?

_____

F. What did God do to Jesus on the cross (Isaiah 53:6)?

_____

III. The Provisions of Christ's Work

Jesus Christ came to earth to pay the price for sin. That price was His own life, which He gave voluntarily (John 10:11,17-18). His sacrifice was the only way to take away sin for all time (Hebrews 9:12).

Describe what Jesus' death accomplished:

A. 1 Peter 3:18 _____

_____

B. Romans 5:10 _____

_____

C. 2 Corinthians 5:21 _____

_____

D. Galatians 1:4 _____

_____

E. Ephesians 1:7 _____

_____

F. Romans 6:6-7 _____

_____

Jesus Christ: The Answer to All Man's Problems Concerning Salvation

Christ's work on the cross and resurrection are the only solution to man's problems. That is why Peter could proclaim of Jesus Christ:

"And there is salvation in no one else; for there is no other name under heaven that has been given among men, by which we must be saved."

Acts 4:12

Refer to your answers in section one of this homework and note how Christ is the answer to each of man's problems.

Man's Problem	The Solution in Christ	Scripture
A. Things man is guilty of: 1. None righteous	"Through the obedience of the One the many will be righteous."	Romans 5:19
2. None understands	"The Son of God has come, and has given us understanding."	1 John 5:20
3. None seeks for God	"The Son of Man has come to seek and to save that which was lost."	Luke 19:10
4. All turned aside	"You were ... straying ... but now you have returned to the Shepherd."	1 Peter 2:25
5. Have become useless	"These qualities ... render you neither useless nor unfruitful ... in Christ."	2 Peter 1:8
6. None do good	"For we are His workmanship, created in Christ Jesus for good works."	Ephesians 2:10
B. Slaves to sin	"Jesus has set you free from the law of sin and of death."	Romans 8:2
C. Facing death	"He who hears My word, and believes Him who sent Me, has eternal life."	John 5:24
D. Facing wrath of God	"Justified by His blood, we shall be saved from the wrath of God through Him."	Romans 5:9

IV. The Motive for Christ's Work

A. Why did God save men (John 3:16 and Romans 5:8)?

_____

B. What attribute of God is demonstrated in His salvation of men (1 Peter 1:3)?

_____

Why does the author call his mercy great? (Hint: Romans 5:6,8)

_____

_____

V. The Resolution and Continuation of Christ's Work

Christ's death on Calvary finished His redemptive work for man (John 19:30). But salvation's story does not end there. The grave could not hold Christ; He lives and continues the work He began for us.

A. How was Christ declared to be the Son of God (Romans 1:4)?

_____

B. After Christ made purification of sins how was He exalted (Hebrews 1:3)?

_____

C. We experience (spiritual) death through Adam's sin. What benefit do we gain through Christ's resurrection (1 Corinthians 15:21-22)?

_____

> The Bible refers to Christ's resurrection as "the first fruits." That is an Old Testament term that speaks of the "first fruits" of the harvest that were set apart for the Lord. When used in the New Testament, "first fruits" implies a pledge of more harvest to follow. Therefore, Christ's resurrection holds the promise of resurrection for others also (1 Corinthians 15:20-22; 1 Peter 1:3).

D. Now that we have been drawn to God through Christ, what is Jesus able to do (Hebrews 7:25)?

_____

E. What role does Christ have exclusively to Himself (1 Timothy 2:5)?

_____

F. When Jesus was going to leave, what did He promise He would do (John 14:3)?

_____

VI. Application

When some people are confronted with the reality of who Christ is, they realize they have made a terrible error in what they believed or how they lived. They are deeply convicted in their hearts in the same way as the men in Jerusalem were when their eyes were opened to the truth:

> *"Now when they heard this, they were pierced to the heart, and said to Peter and the rest of the apostles, 'Brethren, what shall we do?'"*
>
> Acts 2:37

What can you do?

In your heart ...

- ◆ Acknowledge that you have sinned and are not acceptable to God.

- ◆ Repent and call upon the name of Jesus to save you.

- ◆ Seek forgiveness through His blood shed for you.

- ◆ Acknowledge that He is the rightful ruler of your life.

- ◆ Thank God for His love and grace.

❏ I have repented of my sins and called upon the name of Jesus Christ, receiving Him as Lord and Savior.

❏ I have not received Christ but I am still earnestly seeking.

Salvation
Lesson 6 Homework

> Memorize: Ephesians 2:8-10
>
> *"For by grace you have been saved through faith; and that not of yourselves, it is the gift of God; not as a result of works, that no one should boast. For we are His workmanship, created in Christ Jesus for good works, which God prepared beforehand, that we should walk in them."*
>
> Ephesians 2:8-10

How is Christ's redeeming work applied to man? How do we know if someone is a Christian? God has decreed or ordained a plan of salvation that He has revealed to us in the Bible. In this lesson, we will learn how He saves those who believe.

I. God's Sovereignty in Salvation

A. God's Sovereign Plan of Salvation

1. Look at Romans 8:29-30. Write out the progression of how God brings someone to salvation:

verse 29: whom He _____ He also _____

verse 30: whom He _____ He also _____

verse 30: whom He _____ He also _____

verse 30: whom He _____ He also _____

2. Read Ephesians 1:4-6 and answer the following:

a. What has been God's plan before the foundation of the world (verse 4)?

_____

b. What is the purpose of His plan of salvation (verse 6)?

_____

> Grace is "God's free and sovereign act of love and mercy in granting salvation through the death and resurrection of Jesus, apart from anything men are or can do, and of His sustaining that salvation to glorification."
>
> John MacArthur

B. God Implements His Plan of Salvation

> **God's Decree to Reveal His Plan**
>
> *"The mystery which has been kept secret for long ages past, but now is manifested ... according to the commandment of the eternal God, has been made known to all the nations, leading to obedience of faith."*
>
> Romans 16:25-26

1. What does God (the Holy Spirit) do concerning sin (John 16:8)?

   _____

2. Why is the conviction of sin necessary (Jeremiah 17:9; Romans 3:10-19)?

   _____

3. What is needed before someone can know the truth (2 Timothy 2:25)?

   _____

4. Who grants it? _____

5. Read John 1:12-13. Who grants us the right to become children of God

   (verse 12)? _____

> Notice that this right or privilege is not granted to us because of:
>
> - our birth ("born not of blood")
> - our own efforts ("will of the flesh")
> - our own volition ("will of man")

6. Who causes growth in a believer (1 Corinthians 3:6)? _____

7. Who will cause the resurrection to occur (1 Corinthians 6:14)? _____

C. God Culminates His Plan

1. Look again at Romans 8:29. Into whose image will we be ultimately

   conformed? _____

2. What is going to happen to every believer (Philippians 3:20-21)? _____

   _____

   _____

3. What is Christ's desire for those who are His (John 17:24)? _____

_____

II. Conversion

In Numbers 21:5-9, it is recorded how the children of Israel sinned against God, so God sent deadly snakes that bit them and caused death. The people realized their sin and asked to be delivered. God instructed Moses to put a fiery bronze serpent on a pole and when someone was bit, they could look on it and be saved. In a way, that illustrates conversion; however, instead of a snake on a pole, we have the Son of God on a cross.

A. Conviction of Sin

1. What has God given to man to reveal man's sinfulness (Romans 3:20)?

_____

2. When the people realized the mistake they made in crucifying Christ, how did they feel in their hearts (Acts 2:36-37)? _____

_____

B. Repentance from Sin

1. Why did the tax-gatherer cry out to God in the temple (Luke 18:13)?

_____

2. Read 2 Corinthians 7:9-10.

a. What does godly sorrow over sin produce (verse 10)?

_____

b. What does it lead to (verse 10)?

_____

Repentance means a turning away from sin and turning to God.

C. Turning to Christ

When a person who had been bitten by a deadly snake looked at the serpent on the pole, he or she was exercising faith in what God said.

   1. What promise is given to those who call upon the name of the Lord

      (Romans 10:13)? _____

   2. Read Romans 10:8-10. Faith is required for salvation.

     a. What must you confess (verse 9)? _____

     b. What must you believe (verse 9)? _____

**Faith means trusting in, clinging to, or embracing
Jesus Christ who is the object of our faith.**

D. Becoming Slaves to Righteousness

   1. Read Romans 8:1-2.

     a. For the believer in Christ, what is the penalty for sin (verse 1)? _____

     _____

     b. From what is the believer free (verse 2)? _____ and

     _____

   2. When freed from sin, what does a believer become (Romans 6:18)?

     _____

   3. What benefit results (Romans 6:22)? _____

     _____

Sanctification is the process of being conformed to the image of Jesus Christ.

III. Evidence of Salvation

Three important evidences of a true believer are: *faith* that works, *love* that labors, and *hope* that endures (1 Thessalonians 1:3-4).

A. Faith that Works

    1. What reveals genuine faith?

      a. James 2:18 _____

      b. 1 Peter 1:6-7 _____

    2. For what did God prepare believers (Ephesians 2:10)? _____

    3. According to Hebrews 10:39, those with "true faith" will _____

    _____

B. Love that Labors

    1. Besides faith, what else does God take note of in the believer (Hebrews 6:10)?

    _____

    2. What is the source of love in the life of a believer (Romans 5:5)?

    _____

    3. What is true of a person who is born of God (1 John 4:7-8)?

    _____

    4. How does a true believer show love (1 John 3:18-19)? _____

    _____

C. Hope that Endures

    1. Who does Jesus say will be saved (Matthew 10:22)? _____

    _____

    2. What gives us our motivation to endure (1 Timothy 4:10)? _____

    _____

    3. Describe the hope that a Christian has:

      a. Galatians 5:5 _____

      b. 1 Thessalonians 5:8 _____

      c. Titus 3:7 _____

D. The Three that Abide

What three things did Paul notice about the Colossians (Colossians 1:4-5)?

1. _____

2. _____

3. _____

IV. Application

God is sovereign in salvation. The believer is not called to salvation because of his or her own worthiness but because of God's purpose and grace (Ephesians 1:3-14).

A. Realizing that God has chosen you for salvation, how should you respond

(Romans 12:1-2)? _____

B. What is the wrong response (Romans 6:1)? _____

_____

The true believer will be convicted of sin and turn from it. He will be willing to submit to God and follow Christ. A true believer will exhibit:

◆ A Faith that Works

◆ A Love that Labors

◆ A Hope that Endures

Those three qualities are present in every true believer and shape the direction of his or her life.

Look at Psalm 116:16-17. Starting today, what application can you make?

_____

_____

_____

_____

The Person and Ministry of the Holy Spirit
Lesson 7 Homework

Memorize: John 14:16

"And I will ask the Father, and He will give you another Helper, that He may be with you forever."

John 14:16

The Holy Spirit is God. The Bible identifies Him as one of three Persons existing as one God, that is, God the Father, God the Son, and God the Holy Spirit. In this lesson, we will study who the Holy Spirit is and His presence and ministry in the believer's life.

I. The Holy Spirit Is a Person

A. Recognized as a Person

Personal pronouns like "He" or "Him" are used to refer to the Holy Spirit rather than "it." List the number of times "He" or "Him" is used in John 14:17 to refer to the Holy Spirit: _____

B. Attributes of Personality

1. Intellect. He possesses the ability to know and understand reality.

   a. Romans 8:27: The Holy Spirit has a _____ .

   b. 1 Corinthians 2:10: The Holy Spirit searches _____

   _____ .

   c. 1 Corinthians 2:11: The Holy Spirit knows _____

   _____ .

2. Emotion. He possesses the ability to experience emotion.

   Record the emotion attributed to the Holy Spirit in Ephesians 4:30:

   _____

3. Volition. He possesses the ability to determine or act decisively.

List the decision or judgment in which the Holy Spirit demonstrates His attribute of volition:

a. 1 Corinthians 12:7,11 _____

_____

b. Acts 13:2 _____

_____

_____

c. Acts 15:28-29_____

_____

_____

II. The Holy Spirit Is God

A. Attributes

Holy Spirit: Attributes of Deity		
Omniscient	All-knowing	Isaiah 40:13-14
Omnipresent	Present everywhere	Psalm 139:7
Eternal	Without beginning or end	Hebrews 9:14
Truth	Veracity; integrity	1 John 5:7; John 16:13

B. Statements of Deity

1. Write the key statement that shows that the Holy Spirit is God (2 Corinthians 3:17):

_____

2. According to Acts 5:3-4, lying to the Holy Spirit is the same thing as lying to

_____.

III. The Work of the Holy Spirit

A. According to Psalm 104:30, the Holy Spirit is active in _____.

B. 2 Peter 1:20-21 tells us that the Holy Spirit was also active in

_____.

The Holy Spirit Bears Witness of Christ

- ◆ Attests that Jesus is the Christ .... John 15:26
- ◆ Will disclose or reveal Christ .... John 16:14
- ◆ Will not speak of Himself............... John 16:13

IV. The Ministry of the Holy Spirit in Salvation

One of the most important areas of the Spirit's work is with respect to God's plan of salvation.

A. What special work does the Holy Spirit do (John 16:7-8)?

_____

_____

B. By whom are sinners born into God's kingdom (John 3:5-8)?

_____

C. What work does the Spirit do when a person is saved?

1. Titus 3:5-6 _____

_____

2. 1 Corinthians 12:13 _____

_____

The baptism by the Spirit occurs only once—at the time of salvation.

D. How does the Holy Spirit guarantee a believer's salvation (Ephesians 1:13-14)?

_____

The Sealing of the Holy Spirit

A seal was an ancient device, usually a signet ring or cylinder seal engraved with the owner's name or with a particular design, used to seal goods, demonstrate ownership, attest a document's authenticity, or impress an early form of a trademark.

The seal indicated ownership and security. It is the guarantee of future blessings. The presence of the Holy Spirit in our lives is God's promise of our inheritance in the future! What a wonderful assurance.

V. The Ministry of the Holy Spirit in the Believer's Life

A. What is the relationship between the Holy Spirit and the believer (Romans 8:9)?

_____

B. Is it possible to be a Christian and not be indwelled by the Holy Spirit?

_____

C. What is another ministry of the Holy Spirit in the life of the believer

(1 Corinthians 2:12-13)? _____

_____

D. What exhortation is given to all believers in regard to the Spirit?

1. Ephesians 4:30 _____

2. 1 Thessalonians 5:19 _____

3. Ephesians 5:18 _____

Being Filled with the Holy Spirit

To be filled with the Spirit is to "be under His total domination and control."

"To be filled with the Spirit involves confession of sin, surrender of will, intellect, body, time, talent, possessions, and desires. It requires the death of selfishness and the slaying of self-will."

"To be filled with God's Spirit is to be filled with His Word. And as we are filled with God's Word, it controls our thinking and action."

John MacArthur, Jr.

D. How does a Christian keep from sinning (Galatians 5:16)?

_____

E. When a believer is filled with the Holy Spirit, he (the believer) will exhibit the fruit of the Spirit. Examine Galatians 5:22-23 and list these qualities below:

1. _____   6. _____

2. _____   7. _____

3. _____   8. _____

4. _____   9. _____

5. _____

Note: Are you exhibiting those qualities in your own life?

VI. Application

In 1 Corinthians 6:19-20 the Apostle Paul writes:

"Or do you not know that your body is a temple of the Holy Spirit who is in you, whom you have from God, and that you are not your own? For you have been bought with a price: therefore glorify God in your body."

A. What significance does that have for you?

_____

_____

_____

_____

_____

B. What do you need to do to glorify God in your body?

_____

_____

_____

_____

_____

Prayer and the Believer

Lesson 8 Homework

Memorize: Philippians 4:6-7

"Be anxious for nothing, but in everything by prayer and supplication with thanksgiving let your requests be made known to God. And the peace of God, which surpasses all comprehension, shall guard your hearts and your minds in Christ Jesus."

Philippians 4:6-7

The purpose of prayer is to express our submission to the sovereignty of God and our trust in His faithfulness. Prayer is the means by which we express all that is in our hearts to our loving and wise heavenly Father. Prayer is not to give God information, because God knows everything. Prayer brings us into reverent communion with God, worshipping Him and acknowledging Him as the Giver of all things.

I. The Nature of Prayer

A. For the believer, prayer is a learning experience that must be developed into a spiritual discipline.

1. What did the disciples ask of Jesus (Luke 11:1)?

_____

2. Read Romans 8:26.

a. According to the Apostle Paul, who assists us in our prayers?

_____

b. In light of that, what should we do when we are not sure what to pray for?

_____

B. Prayer is an exchange of intimacy with God. The Scripture tells us God is very interested in our personal struggles.

1. What does Psalm 34:15 say about the Lord?

_____

2. What did David bring before God in prayer (Psalm 142:2)?

_____

3. How are we encouraged to approach God (Hebrews 4:16)?

_____

4. Though we have the privilege of access, what caution does Ecclesiastes 5:1-2 advise?

_____

5. What comfort does 1 Peter 5:6-7 offer believers?

_____

_____

C. Prayer is effective. Prayer can change situations—and people. We are encouraged to pray expecting results.

1. For whom did the church pray in Acts 12:5?

_____

2. How did God answer their prayers (Acts 12:7)?

_____

3. Besides answers, what else does God grant to those who pray (Philippians 4:6-7)?

_____

_____

> *"The effective prayer of a righteous man can accomplish much."*
> James 5:16b

II. The Practice of Prayer

A. Throughout the Bible, God encourages and commands believers to persevere in prayer.

1. In Luke 18:1, the disciples were taught that they should always pray, and not

_____

2. What is God's will for believers in Christ Jesus (1 Thessalonians 5:17)?

_____

3. When should believers pray (Ephesians 6:18)?

_____

B. The Bible is God's handbook on prayer. In it you will discover many guidelines to help you develop the practice of prayer.

1. What did Jesus teach His disciples to expect if they persisted in prayer (Luke 11:5-10)?

_____

_____

2. What does Jesus teach as a requirement for answered prayer (John 15:7)?

_____

3. According to 1 John 5:14, what is our confidence as we pray?

_____

Jesus' Pattern for Prayer: Matthew 6:9-13

Pray to God ....Our Father Who art in heaven
Exalt Him saying ....Hallowed be Thy name
Submit to Him praying ....Thy Kingdom come, Thy will be done
Look to Him seeking ....Our daily bread (sustenance)
Confess to Him pleading ....Forgive us our debts (sins)
Depend on Him asking ....Lead us not into temptation
Trust in Him requesting .... Deliver us from evil

C. Look up the following verses and list some of the hinderances to answered prayer.

    1. Psalm 66:18 _____

    2. James 4:3 _____

    _____

    3. 1 Peter 3:7 _____

    _____

Four Important Areas of Prayer

Adoration   Reflect on God Himself. Praise Him for His attributes, His majesty, His gift of Christ.

Confession   Admit to God you have sinned. Be honest and humble. Remember, He knows you and loves you.

Thanksgiving   Tell God how grateful you are for everything He has given you, even the unpleasant things. Your thankfulness will help you see His purposes.

Supplication   Make specific requests. Pray for others first, then for yourself.

Notice the first letters of these four words form the word "ACTS."
Use them as a mental guide to maintain balance as you pray.

III. The Struggle of Prayer

    A. Prayer can be hard work. That should not keep us from praying, even when it requires sacrifice.

        1. How long did Jesus pray before He selected the twelve apostles (Luke 6:12)?

        _____

2. Describe the intensity of Jesus as He prayed in the garden (Luke 22:44).

_____

3. What should believers be careful to do when we devote ourselves to prayer (Colossians 4:2)?

_____

_____

B. Even when we are frustrated or discouraged, we can still approach God in prayer.

1. Why was David discouraged (Psalm 13:1-2)?

_____

2. What was David's complaint in Psalm 22:2?

_____

C. Prayer is governed by God's sovereignty, and His purpose determines His answer to our prayers.

1. Read 2 Corinthians 12:7-9.

a. What did Paul pray for?

_____

b. How many times did he pray for it?

_____

c. Did he receive what he asked for? Why or why not?

_____

2. Read Mark 14:35-36.

a. What did Jesus ask of the Father concerning His "hour" of suffering?

_____

_____

b. Yet, what was He willing to do?

_____

IV. Application

Compose a simple prayer following the ACTS model on page 56.

_____

_____

_____

_____

_____

_____

_____

_____

_____

_____

_____

_____

_____

_____

_____

> Surrender your requests to God's wise and loving plan, acknowledging
> your willingness to receive His answer with thankfulness.

The Church: Fellowship and Worship

Lesson 9 Homework

Memorize: Hebrews 10:24-25

"And let us consider how to stimulate one another to love and good deeds, not forsaking our own assembling together, as is the habit of some, but encouraging one another; and all the more, as you see the day drawing near."

Hebrews 10:24-25

I. The Church Universal

"The Church is not a physical building, but a group of believers; not a denomination, sect, or association, but a spiritual Body. The Church is not an organization, but ... a communion, a fellowship that includes all believers."

John F. MacArthur, Jr.

A. Read Colossians 1:18 and Ephesians 5:23.

1. What is Christ's position in the church? _____

2. How is the church described? _____

B. At what cost did Christ purchase the church (Acts 20:28)?

_____

C. How does a person become a member of the body of Christ?

1. Colossians 3:15. We are _____ into the body.

2. 1 Corinthians 12:13. We are _____ into the body.

II. The Local Church

The New Testament decribes how believers came together in small groups to worship Christ, receive instruction from the Scriptures, meet one another's needs, pray, and evangelize.

A. The Local Church Illustrated

   1. Where did the believers meet before they had church buildings (Romans 16:5; 1 Corinthians 16:19)?

   _____

   2. On what day of the week did they meet (Acts 20:7)?

   _____

   3. List four things to which the early church was devoted (Acts 2:42):

   a. _____   c. _____

   b. _____   d. _____

B. The Local Church Organized

   1. In Ephesians 4:11-12, God gave gifted men to the church.

   a. List them: _____

   _____

   _____

   _____

   b. God gave these gifted men to the church to equip the saints for what purposes (verse 12)?

   _____

   _____

2. Elders/Overseers

   a. The qualifications of an elder or overseer are stated in 1 Timothy 3:1-7 and Titus 1:6-9.

   b. What are the two major responsibilities of an elder (1 Peter 5:1-2)?

      (1) _____

      (2) _____

   c. What is the responsibility of believers to the elders (Hebrews 13:17)?

      _____

3. Deacons

   The word "deacon" means "servant." The deacons are to minister to the needs of the flock under the direction of the elders of the church. The qualifications of deacons are stated in 1 Timothy 3:8-13.

4. Members of the body

   a. What does Hebrews 10:25 warn believers not to neglect?

      _____

   b. Hebrews 13:7 instructs us concerning those who teach us God's Word. What should be our response? (Circle the correct answer.)

      (1) That we should encourage others to come and hear them.
      (2) That we should not hope to have the kind of faith they have.
      (3) That we should observe their godly lives and follow their example of faith.

   c. How should we act toward other members of the body (1 Corinthians 12:25)?

      _____

5. How should those who are appointed to preach and teach be supported?

   a. 1 Corinthians 9:14 _____

   b. Galatians 6:6 _____

III. Fellowship

The Bible uses the Greek word *koinonia* to describe fellowship within the body of Christ. That word means "participation with others in a common purpose." The Latin equivalent is *communion,* pointing to the communion that is shared with other believers as well as with God.

A. What is God's desire for every local church (1 Corinthians 1:10)?

_____

B. In Ephesians 4:2-3:

1. What will promote unity (verse 2)? _____

_____

2. What is our responsibility (verse 3)? _____

_____

C. Read Philippians 2:1-4. What is the key to maintaining unity within the body (verse 3)?

_____

_____

D. Scripture is clear that the believer enjoys fellowship with:

1. God the Father . . . . 1 John 1:3
2. God the Son . . . . 1 John 1:3
3. Holy Spirit . . . . 2 Corinthians 13:14
4. Other believers . . . . 1 John 1:7

However, with whom is true fellowship not possible (2 Corinthians 6:14-15)?

_____

E. Fellowship within the body of Christ involves sharing in each other's lives. Below are some areas in which Christians should minister to one another:

1. Romans 14:19 _____

2. Galatians 5:13 _____

3. Galatians 6:2 _____

4. James 5:16 _____

F. What has God given to each Christian to help him or her minister to others within the church (1 Peter 4:10-11)?

_____

IV. Worship

The English word "worship" was originally spelled "worthship," meaning to acknowledge the worth of someone or something. We worship when we give honor to God for who He is. Worship acknowledges God's Person, nature, attributes, and works. It stems from a grateful heart and renders adoration, devotion, and submission to God.

A. God seeks genuine worshipers.

Read John 4:23-24. How are we to worship God (verse 24)?

_____

> If we are to worship God in truth (i.e., not in error), we must seek to know Him by learning about His attributes and actions.

B. We worship God because only He is worthy of our highest devotion. Read Revelation 4:10-11 and answer the following:

1. What is God worthy to receive?

_____

2. Why? _____

C. Worshiping God involves praise.

How did the psalmist say God should be worshiped (Psalm 66:4)?

_____

D. Worshiping God involves reverence.

1. What did Moses do when he worshiped God (Exodus 34:8)?

_____

2. How is reverence for God revealed in the following verses?

a. Exodus 34:8 _____

b. Luke 7:1-7 _____

c. Revelation 1:17 _____

"O come, let us sing for joy to the Lord;
Let us shout joyfully to the rock of our salvation.
Let us come before His presence with thanksgiving;
Let us shout joyfully to Him with psalms.
For the Lord is a great God,
And a great King above all gods,
In whose hand are the depths of the earth;
The peaks of the mountains are His also.
The sea is His, for it was He who made it;
And His hands formed the dry land.
Come, let us worship and bow down;
Let us kneel before the Lord our Maker."

Psalm 95:1-6

THE LORD'S SUPPER

The Lord's Supper, or Communion, is one of two ordinances given to the church by Jesus Christ, the other being baptism. The Lord's Supper is an act of remembrance of Christ's death.

Read 1 Corinthians 11:23-26 and write the answers to the following:

1. The bread is in remembrance of _____

2. The cup is in remembrance of _____

3. Every time you partake in Communion you proclaim the Lord's death (1 Corinthians 11:26). In light of that truth, what is the warning stated in 1 Corinthians 11:27-30?

   _____

   _____

   _____

V. Application

A. Are you a member of the body of Christ? _____

B. Are you a member of a local assembly of Christians? _____

C. What have you learned from this study to improve your worship of God?

   _____

   _____

   _____

   _____

Spiritual Gifts

Lesson 10 Homework

Memorize: 1 Corinthians 12:7

"But to each one is given the manifestation of the Spirit for the common good."

1 Corinthians 12:7

Spiritual gifts are given by God to believers for the purpose of ministry within the church. The English term comes from two Greek words, *charismata* and *pneumatika*. The root of *charismata* is *charis*, which means "grace" and speaks of something undeserved or unearned. The second word, *pneumatika*, means "spirituals" or things given by the Spirit of God. In this lesson, you will look at various spiritual gifts and how they should be used in the body of Christ.

I. The Nature of Spiritual Gifts

A. Who is the source of spiritual giftedness?

    1. 1 Corinthians 12:11 _____

    2. 1 Corinthians 12:28 _____

B. Who possesses spiritual giftedness (1 Peter 4:10)?

_____

C. What is the purpose of spiritual gifts?

    1. 1 Corinthians 12:4-7 _____

    2. 1 Corinthians 14:12 _____

    3. 1 Peter 4:10-11 _____

_____

II. The Provision of Spiritual Gifts

A. Spiritual gifts are referred to in Scripture. List them below:

1. 1 Corinthians 12:8-10

_____   _____   _____

_____   _____   _____

_____   _____   _____

2. 1 Corinthians 12:28b

_____   _____   _____

_____   _____

3. Romans 12:6-8

_____   _____   _____

_____   _____

_____   _____

B. Understanding the gifts.

For a better understanding of how the spiritual gifts function, we have classified the gifts into two categories: temporary (special) and permanent.

TEMPORARY GIFTS
Temporary gifts were given by the Holy Spirit for confirming the testimony of the apostles and prophets. They were prevalent in the early church, but ceased to be evident as the church was established.

■ **Miracles**

The ability to do "wonders" and "signs." Christ performed many miracles as recorded in Scripture. Paul used this gift to affirm his apostleship as described in 2 Corinthians 12:12.

■ **Healing**

Peter had this gift (see Acts 3:6-8; 5:15-16), which affirmed his message and helped establish the foundation for the church.

■ **Tongues and Interpretation of Tongues**

Manifested by the speaking of a language unknown to the speaker (see Acts 2:1-11). This gift had to be accompanied by the gift of interpretation (1 Corinthians 14:27-28).

PERMANENT GIFTS

Gifts given by the Holy Spirit for the building up of the church.
These were prevalent in the early church and still are in the church today.

■ **Prophecy**

Preaching or "to tell forth or declare the Scripture." Prophecy does not necessarily mean to foretell the future.

■ **Teaching**

The ability to teach the Word of God and bless the hearers with the understanding of the Scriptures that the Author intended.

■ **Faith**

A consistent, enabling faith that truly believes God in the face of overwhelming obstacles and human impossibilities, and for great things. John MacArthur calls this the "gift of prayer" because the gift is primarily expressed toward God through prayer.

■ **Wisdom**

The ability to apply wisdom, gained from spiritual insight, to believers; knowing what is right and what is wrong; applied knowledge.

■ **Knowledge**

An understanding of the facts of Scripture. From the human perspective, it is scholarship or the ability to know the truths of Scripture in a way that is both broad and deep.

■ **Discernment**

The ability to tell which things are from the Spirit and which are not; distinguishes truth from error. This gift serves as protection for the church.

■ **Mercy**

The ability to show deep compassion to those who have spiritual, physical, or emotional needs.

■ **Exhortation**

The ability to encourage and motivate. A person with this gift can come alongside another to comfort him with love, to encourage him to a deeper spiritual commitment and growth, or to exhort him to action. This is the gift that qualifies people to exercise a counseling ministry in the body.

■ **Giving**

This gift is a direct reference to the material ministry of giving: food, clothes, money, houses, etc. in response to the needs of the church.

■ **Administration/Leadership**

The ability to oversee the flock. This may be seen in pastors and elders; also those in leadership of missionary societies, youth work, evangelistic associations, etc.

■ **Helps**

Aiding in a time of need, or bearing one another's burdens, as the situation arises.

■ Service

Working for the body of Christ in areas of physical ministries such as serving food, maintenance, etc.

Evangelism and the Believer
Lesson 11 Homework

Memorize: 1 Peter 3:15

"But sanctify Christ as Lord in your hearts, always being ready to make a defense to everyone who asks you to give an account for the hope that is in you, yet with gentleness and reverence."

1 Peter 3:15

The word *evangelism* brings many thoughts to mind. Some think of tents and famous speakers; still others of weekly "visitation" and the terror of "witnessing." This lesson will introduce the biblical concept of evangelism and the role the believer plays.

I. The Call to Evangelism

A. According to Mark 16:15, what were the disciples to do?

_____

B. What are three aspects of making disciples recorded in Matthew 28:19-20?

1. _____

2. _____

3. _____

C. What did Jesus say should be proclaimed to all the nations (Luke 24:46-47)?

_____

_____

D. What was Paul to tell all people (Acts 22:15)?

_____

_____

II. The Good News of Evangelism: The Gospel

A. According to 1 Corinthians 15:3-4, what is the good news that Paul preached?

1. _____

2. _____

3. _____

B. Of what did Paul say he was not ashamed (Romans 1:16)?

_____

Why? _____

_____

III. The Essentials of Evangelism

A. What must someone believe about Jesus Christ for salvation?

1. John 1:1 _____

2. John 14:6 _____

3. Acts 4:12 _____

B. The following are key verses in sharing the gospel message. Look up each verse and briefly summarize the key point:

1. Romans 3:23 _____

2. Romans 6:23 _____

3. Romans 5:8 _____

4. 1 Peter 2:24 _____

5. Romans 10:9 _____

_____

6. John 1:12 _____

Most People Do Not Understand the Following:

- Man cannot save himself . . . . Mark 10:26-27
- God is holy, righteous, and hates sin . . . . Psalm 5:4-5
- Jesus Christ is God . . . . Colossians 2:9
- Christ's death on the cross was for our sins . . . . 1 Peter 3:18
- Christ offers heaven as a free gift of God . . . . Romans 6:23

IV. Strategy for Evangelism

A. Witness by your life

1. What kind of life should we live and how should we appear to the world (Philippians 2:14-15)?

_____

_____

Others Will See Your Redeemer Through Your Redeemed Life.

2. Read Matthew 5:16.

a. What do people notice that makes a Christian's life shine?

_____

_____

b. What will be the result? _____

_____

3. According to Colossians 4:6, how should you speak to others?

_____

B. Prayer

1. As Paul prayed for others, what was on his heart (Romans 10:1)?

_____

2. For what requests did Paul ask the Colossians to pray (Colossians 4:3-4)?

_____

_____

3. When speaking the Word of God to others, especially in threatening situations, what should we ask God to give us (Acts 4:29)?

_____

> "First of all, then, I urge that entreaties and prayers, petitions and thanksgivings, be made on behalf of all men.... This is good and acceptable in the sight of God our Savior, who desires all men to be saved and to come to the knowledge of the truth."
>
> 1 Timothy 2:1,3-4

C. Use God's Word

1. What will God's Word do (Hebrews 4:12)?

_____

_____

2. How did Paul use the Scripture in witnessing (Acts 17:2-3)?

_____

_____

3. What are the Scriptures able to do (2 Timothy 3:15)?

_____

_____

We must be ready to speak of Christ in any situation. We must know the essentials of the gospel. We must have confidence in God and His Word.

"Always being ready to make a defense ... to give an account for the hope that is in you" (1 Peter 3:15).

Then pray and look for opportunities!

V. Application

List several people whom you want to reach for Christ. Pray regularly for those people and prepare for the opportunity to share the Word of God with them. Allow God to do His convicting work and trust Him.

1. _____

2. _____

3. _____

4. _____

5. _____

Remember, Exemplify Christlikeness.

Witness to those people with your lives, and your message will be more clearly understood!

Obedience

Lesson 12 Homework

> Memorize: 1 John 2:3-4
>
> *"And by this we know that we have come to know Him, if we keep His commandments. The one who says, 'I have come to know Him,' and does not keep His commandments, is a liar, and the truth is not in him."*
>
> 1 John 2:3-4

Obedience is more than following a set of rules. It is the expected response of a Christian to his Lord. In this lesson, we will study what it means to be obedient, areas of obedience, and some results of obedience.

I. The Call to Obedience

> *"As obedient children ... like the Holy One who called you, be holy yourselves also in all your behavior."*
>
> 1 Peter 1:14-15

A. The Call to Obey God's Commands

1. According to John 14:15, Jesus said, "If you love Me, you will _____

_____."

2. What is expected of those who hear God's Word (James 1:22)?

_____

B. The Call to Follow Christ

1. What is required of a person who follows Jesus (Luke 9:23)?

a. _____

b. _____

c. _____

2. How did Jesus set the example for us when suffering for His obedience to God (1 Peter 2:20-23)?

_____

Obedience is not merely following a list of "dos and don'ts." It involves following Jesus Christ and seeking after the things above.

(Note: Colossians 2:20-3:2)

C. The Call to Submission

"Do you not know that when you present yourselves to someone as slaves for obedience, you are slaves of the one whom you obey, either of sin resulting in death, or of obedience resulting in righteousness?" (Romans 6:16)

How should we present ourselves to God (Romans 12:1)?

_____

_____

II. Obedience Marks a True Believer

A. Look at 1 John 2:3-4 (memory verse).

1. What does obeying the Word of God demonstrate?

_____

2. What does continuous disobedience to the Word of God indicate?

_____

B. What characterizes the true believer as one who will enter the kingdom of heaven (Matthew 7:21)?

_____

"But whoever keeps His word, in him the love of God has truly been perfected. By this we know that we are in Him."

1 John 2:5

80

III. Examples of Disobedience

A. Read 1 Samuel 15:16-23. Instead of complete obedience to God's command, King Saul substituted his own way of worship and excused his disobedience.

    1. What was Samuel's reply? How did he compare obedience and sacrifice (verse 22)?

       _____

    2. To what are stubbornness and rebellion compared (verse 23)?

       _____

    3. What did Saul's disobedience cost him (verse 23)?

       _____

B. Consider Zechariah 7:8-14.

    1. How did the people react to God's instruction (verses 11-12)? _____

       _____

    2. How did it affect their prayers (verse 13)? _____

       _____

    3. What was the result (verse 14)? _____

       _____

IV. Examples of Obedience

The Old Testament contains numerous examples of obedience. Notice the Old Testament heroes of faith and obedience listed in Hebrews 11.

A. Abraham's Obedience

    1. What were two of Abraham's great acts of obedience?

       a. Genesis 12:1-4; Hebrews 11:8 _____

       _____

       b. Genesis 22:1-12 _____

       _____

2. Because Abraham obeyed God, what three things did God promise to Abraham's son (Genesis 26:2-5)?

a. _____

b. _____

c. _____

B. Christ's Example of Obedience

1. What was Christ's primary concern on earth (John 4:34)?

_____

2. Even when facing the cross, what was Christ's attitude (Luke 22:42)?

_____

3. To what extent was Jesus willing to be obedient (Philippians 2:8)?

_____

V. The Promises and Blessings of Obedience

A. List some blessings that are promised to us if we obey God's commandments.

1. John 15:10 _____

2. John 15:14 _____

3. 1 John 3:22 _____

B. To what does Jesus compare the life of a person who hears and obeys His Word (Matthew 7:24-27)?

_____

_____

_____

VI. Areas of Obedience

A. What are all Christians to be taught concerning Christ's commands (Matthew 28:20)?

_____

_____

B. Read each verse below. Fill in who is to be obedient to whom and why.

1. Colossians 3:20

   a. Who?_____ To Whom? _____

   b. Why?_____

   _____

2. Ephesians 5:22-24

   a. Who?_____ To Whom? _____

   b. Why?_____

   _____ (Note: Ephesians 5:25-32)

3. Ephesians 6:5-8

   a. Who?_____ To Whom? _____

   b. Why?_____

   _____

4. Hebrews 13:17

   a. Who?_____ To Whom? _____

   b. Why?_____

   _____

5. Romans 13:1

   a. Who?_____ To Whom? _____

   b. Why?_____

   _____

C. What should a wife do if her husband is an unbeliever (1 Peter 3:1)?

_____

_____

D. What if a servant (or employee) has an "impossible" employer? What should he or she do (1 Peter 2:18-19)?

_____

_____

VII. Our Attitude Toward Obedience

We must remember that all our good works apart from faith are like filthy rags (Isaiah 64:6). Obedience without genuine faith avails nothing. But our obedience must grow out of a heart of sincere faith toward God.

A. What was the basis of all Abraham's obedience (Hebrews 11:8)?

_____

B. Read the "parable of the two sons" (Matthew 21:28-32). Which son had the better attitude? Why?

_____

_____

C. Using Peter as our example, what should be our response when God's Word seems contrary to our own judgment (Luke 5:1-7)?

_____

D. Read Ephesians 6:6.

1. How should we view ourselves in relation to Christ?

_____

2. What should be our attitude in doing all the will of God?

_____

> *"So you too, when you do all the things which are commanded you, say,'We are unworthy slaves; we have done only that which we ought to have done.'"*
>
> Luke 17:10

VIII. Application

A. What does it mean to "present your bodies a living and holy sacrifice, acceptable to God" (Romans 12:1)?

_____

_____

_____

B. What have you learned about the consequences of disobedience?

_____

_____

_____

C. In what areas of your life does God want greater obedience?

_____

_____

_____

God's Will and Guidance

Lesson 13 Homework

Memorize: Ephesians 5:17

"So then do not be foolish, but understand what the will of the Lord is."

Ephesians 5:17

God is sovereign and has a purpose for all of His creation. He has a plan or "will" for each of us and we often make His will more difficult to respond to than it really is. In this lesson we will explore God's will and how we are guided into His will.

I. God's Will

The Bible portrays two aspects of God's will: sovereign will and commanded will. In God's sovereignty, He has a plan that covers all aspects of creation and time. He also has a commanded will that He legislates to His people.

A. The Meaning of God's Will

1. God's sovereign will

   God's sovereign will involves His ultimate, complete control over everything. Nothing happens that was not in God's plan. History is really the unfolding of God's purposes, which happen exactly as He planned.

   Look up the following verses and write out the key thought about God's sovereign will:

   a. Isaiah 14:24 _____

   _____

   _____

   b. Ephesians 1:11b _____

   _____

"I am God, and there is no one like Me.... My purpose will be established, and I will accomplish all My good pleasure."

Isaiah 46:9-10

2. God's commanded will

God's commanded will is revealed throughout the Bible as laws or principles. It is that aspect of His will to which men are held accountable.

a. According to the Great Commission (Matthew 28:20), what are new believers to be taught?

_____

b. God gave two great commandments. List them below:

(1) Matthew 22:37 _____

_____

(2) Matthew 22:39_____

_____

B. The Nature of God's Will

God's sovereign will and commanded will are better understood in light of their respective characteristics.

Sovereign Will	Commanded Will
1. Secret; known only to God except as revealed through history or revelation.	1. Revealed in the Bible.
2. Cannot be resisted or thwarted.	2. Can be resisted or disobeyed.
3. Encompasses both good and evil (sin).	3. Involves only that which is good; holy.
4. Comprehensive; controls all aspects of life, time, and history.	4. Specific; provides principles for living.
5. The believer is not commanded to know or discover what God has not revealed.	5. Believers are exhorted to know, understand, and obey all that God has revealed.

Study the table on the previous page. Test your understanding of God's <u>sovereign will</u> and His <u>commanded will</u>.

- Write out the part of the verse that conveys God's will.
- Check the appropriate box.

	Sovereign Will	Commanded Will
1. Philippians 2:13	❑	❑
2. 1 Thessalonians 4:3	❑	❑
3. 2 Corinthians 6:14	❑	❑
4. Matthew 7:21	❑	❑
5. Philippians 1:6	❑	❑
6. Jeremiah 29:11	❑	❑

C. Response to God's Will

    1. How should we respond to God's sovereign will?

        a. Proverbs 3:5-6 _____

        _____

        b. 1 Peter 4:19 _____

        _____

        c. James 4:13-15 _____

        _____

    2. How should we respond to God's commanded will?

        a. Ephesians 5:17 _____

        _____

        b. Deuteronomy 29:29 _____

        _____

        c. Deuteronomy 11:1 _____

        _____

        _____

God instructs; we obey.

"Good and upright is the Lord;
Therefore He instructs sinners in the way.
He leads the humble in justice,
And He teaches the humble His way.
All the paths of the Lord are lovingkindness and truth
To those who keep His covenant and His testimonies."

Psalm 25:8-10

II. Guidance

Because of His great love, God has predestined, called, justified, and will glorify all believers. He also guides us.

A. Meaning of Guidance

Guidance is God's active role in our lives, accomplishing His purposes.

Note the following words used in the Bible to describe guidance. Write down how the verse conveys the meaning of each word:

1. *Lead* (to shepherd; to bear or carry)

    a. Psalm 78:52 _____

    _____

    b. Psalm 139:24 _____

    _____

2. *Guide* (to show; to help understand)

    a. Psalm 23:3 _____

    _____

    b. Psalm 73:24 _____

    _____

3. *Direct* (to establish or prepare; to make straight)

    a. Proverbs 16:9 _____

    _____

    b. 2 Thessalonians 3:5 _____

    _____

B. The Nature of Guidance

The chart below outlines ways in which God guides people directly or indirectly:

Direct Guidance	Indirect Guidance
1. Spoken revelation from God.	1. God's Word
2. Visions	2. Conscience or conviction
3. Dreams	3. Providence (i.e., circumstances controlled by God)
4. Prophet/Apostle speaking for God.	4. Wisdom and counsel

Direct guidance was experienced during the Old Testament and early New Testament time periods. Today, we see God guiding indirectly. The Holy Spirit is active in all areas of indirect guidance as part of His ministry in the believer.

1. Guidance through God's Word

How does the psalmist describe God's Word (Psalm 119:105)?

_____

2. Guidance through conviction

How was Paul stimulated to action in Athens (Acts 17:16)?

_____

3. Guidance through God's providence

What can the believer be confident about regardless of the circumstances (Romans 8:28)?

_____

_____

4. Guidance through God-given wisdom

    a. Read Proverbs 2:1-11. What four things will wisdom allow you to discern (verse 9)?

        (1) _____

        (2) _____

        (3) _____

        (4) _____

    b. What is the result of seeking counsel (Proverbs 13:10)? _____

III. Application

    A. List one area in which you are wrestling with a decision:

    _____

    _____

    _____

    B. Does this issue involve:

        God's sovereign will?   ❑

        God's commanded will?   ❑

        I don't know which one. ❑

    C. What should your response be if it involves:

        1. God's sovereign will . . . . Proverbs 3:5-6

        2. God's commanded will . . . . John 15:10

        3. You are unsure . . . . James 1:5

    What action are you going to take?

    _____

    _____

    _____

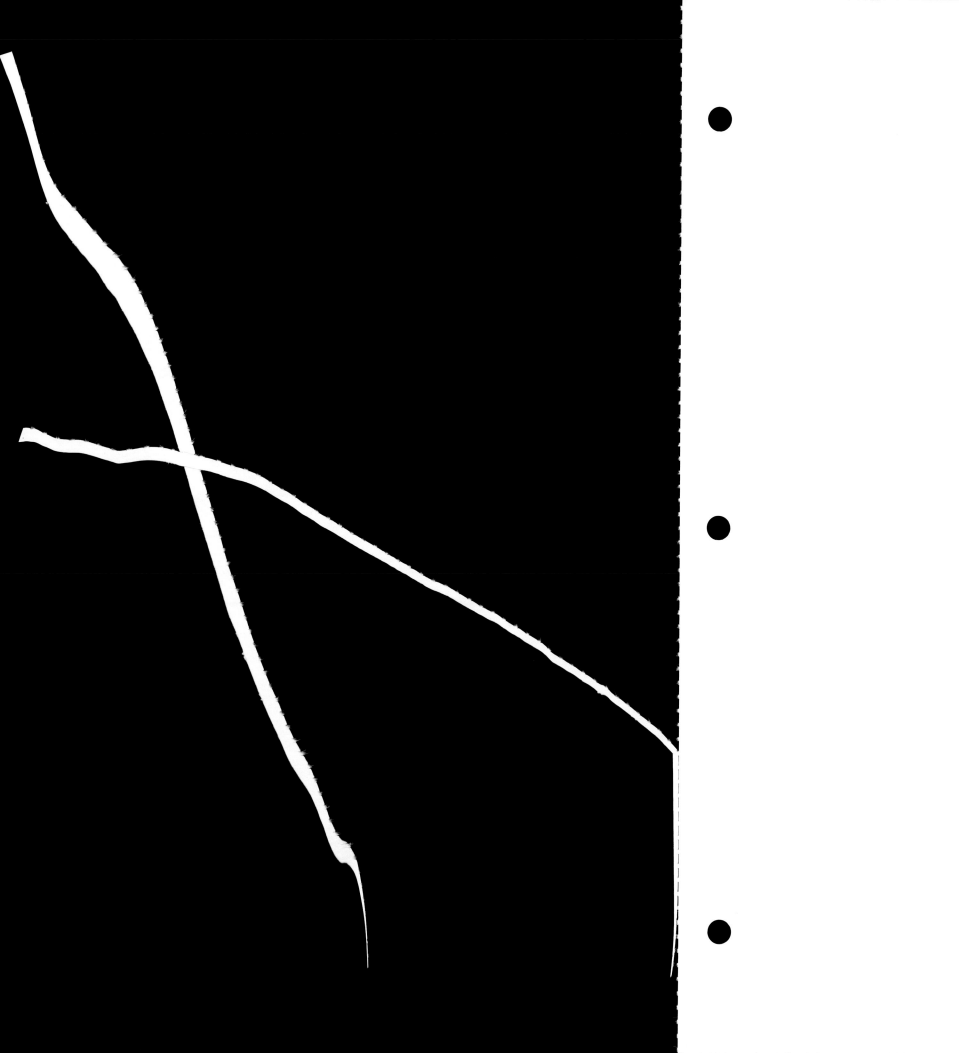